PRAYER
in practice

First published 1986
by the Incorporated Catholic Truth Society
38–40 Eccleston Square, London SW1V 1PD

ISBN 0 85183 651 8   AC

Prayer in Practice originally appeared as
a series of articles in *The Tablet,* and
are © 1985 The Tablet Publishing Co. Ltd.

Printed in Great Britain by
Staples Printers Rochester Limited
at The Stanhope Press

Contents

A Note on the Contributors

DAVID GOODALL, who is a senior official at the Foreign and Commonwealth Office, was born in Lancashire in 1931 and educated at Ampleforth and Trinity College, Oxford. He joined the Diplomatic Service after two years in the army and his overseas postings have included Indonesia, Kenya, Austria and Germany. He is married with three children.

EDWARD YARNOLD SJ was born in 1926 and entered the Society of Jesus in 1943. He was Master of Campion Hall from 1965–72. He is now a tutor there, and Chairman of the Oxford University Faculty of Theology. He was a member of the Anglican-Roman Catholic International Commission (ARCIC) and is now serving on ARCIC-II. He is the author of several books and articles, including *Truth and Authority* and *An ARCIC Catechism* (both with Henry Chadwick), *Eight Days with the Lord* and *The Church and the Churches* (all CTS).

MARGARET HEBBLETHWAITE is co-author of *The Theology of Penance* (Mercier Press, Dublin and Cork, 1979), author of *Motherhood and God* (Geoffrey Chapman, London, 1984) and *Through Lent with Luke* (Bible Reading Fellowship, London, 1986). She is a broadcaster, retreat-giver, and mother of three young children. She is married to the Catholic writer Peter Hebblethwaite.

MARTHA SKINNIDER SND is a Sister of Notre Dame de Namur who lives and works in one of Glasgow's larger peripheral housing schemes.

FELICITAS CORRIGAN OSB is a Benedictine nun of Stanbrook Abbey who has lived an enclosed contemplative life for half a century. She is the author of *The Nun, the Infidel and the Superman* (John Murray, 1985).

GERARD W. HUGHES SJ has taught at Stonyhurst College, was Catholic Chaplain at Glasgow University, and Director of the Jesuit Centre of Spirituality at St Beuno's, North Wales. His latest book is *God of Surprises* (Darton, Longman and Todd, 1985).

PATRICK BARRY OSB was first professed as a Benedictine at Ampleforth in 1936, ordained priest in 1945, was housemaster in the school from 1954 to 1964 and headmaster from 1964 to 1979. Between 1980 and 1984 he was engaged in parish and retreat work in Cardiff and worked with the Worth community in East Dulwich; in April 1984 he was elected Abbot of Ampleforth.

1.

The heart of the matter

David Goodall

What reforms would you most like to see in the Church? Married clergy, women priests, new organisational structures, modification of *Humanae Vitae*, a different kind of pope. Ask this question, and these are the sorts of answer which people give. But there is another answer, which could bring about changes more far-reaching than any of these: the rediscovery of the primacy of prayer.

I am sure that sooner or later every Christian, whatever his condition, comes to realise that the most persuasive – perhaps the only completely persuasive – apologetic for Christian belief is the phenomenon of holiness: that unseen but pervasive presence of God in another person which, once recognised, has an authenticity which it is impossible to refute. There is an infinite variety of routes to holiness, which in the last analysis can only be a gratuitous gift from God. But between holiness and prayer there is an observable connection which suggests that prayer is a primary source of holiness and, for most people, a necessary condition of it. From this observation has sprung the conviction, which has grown stronger over the years, that prayer is the touchstone of the Christian life, crucial to the faith of the individual believer, crucial to the Church's survival and crucial to what the Church is for.

The 'penny catechism' defines prayer as 'the raising up of the mind and heart to God.' It is hard to improve on that lapidary definition. Christian prayer consists fundamentally in making oneself aware of the reality of God, and of adverting to that reality. In other words, prayer is the activity in which we deliberately confront the existence of the personal, unseen God in whom we believe.

This is the case irrespective of whether the particular act of prayer is public or private, collective or individual, audible or silent. We may be asking God for something, praising him, thanking him, listening to him, or simply reflecting on or contemplating him. We may be repenting, or we may be reproaching him; or we may indeed be resisting him – for God can sometimes be encountered most directly in a conflict of wills. But whatever may be its particular form or content, the distinguishing characteristics of Christian prayer are that it is an interior acknowledgment of the reality of the Unseen and an encounter with someone other than oneself. (It is in this respect that Christian meditative prayer differs radically from the various forms of self-improvement which currently go under the name of meditation, and in which the dialogue, if there is one, is with one's 'deepest self'.)

Because the Christian worldview, with its commitment to the unseen and the intangible, is *prima facie* at odds with the world of sense experience which conditions most of our thinking, the practice of prayer – the act of adverting consciously to the unseen reality on which that worldview is based – has always been of central importance for the retention of a Christian perspective. The abandonment or devaluation of prayer has always tended to lead, whether in groups or in individuals, to an erosion of the faith and its reduction to an ethical or political husk. But two important developments, one gradual and one relatively sudden, have brought the importance of prayer into even sharper focus. First, there has been the gradual change in the status of Christianity, from being formally the religion of society as a whole to being the faith of a fragmented minority subsisting within, and partly assimilated to, a non-believing majority. On top of that has come the post-Vatican II reorientation of the Catholic Church in favour of openness to the world, which has involved extensive dismantling of the barriers of custom, rules of behaviour and modes of thought that helped to maintain the cohesion and separateness of the largest of the Christian bodies.

It is not my purpose here to pass any value judgment on these developments, but simply to draw attention to their sociological result. This has been to reduce the community of Christian believers to the status of a deviant minority; and a minority, moreover, which is virtually inviting ideological penetration by the non-believing majority, whose value system is in many respects at variance with the Christian one and to whom the notion of an unseen, personal and loving God is either irrelevant or fanciful.

The implications of this situation for Christian

belief were lucidly explored by Peter Berger in his
celebrated book *A Rumour of Angels* (Penguin Books
1971). Berger reminds us that 'knowledge' has a
social dimension, and that the plausibility or credibility of what we believe or think we know about
the world depends largely on the social support these
beliefs receive: in other words, on the extent to which
other people share them. This means that the beliefs
of a 'cognitive minority' – defined by Berger as 'a
group of people whose worldview differs signifi-
cantly from the one generally taken for granted in
their society' – are highly vulnerable to erosion from
the worldview of the majority.

At first sight, a 'pluralist' society of the kind which
exists today over most of Western Europe and North
America, and which explicitly makes room for a
wide spectrum of conflicting beliefs and attitudes
should be an environment in which it is relatively
easy for minorities to retain their distinctive world-
views. In reality, however, the tolerance which makes
pluralism possible derives from an agnostic ortho-
doxy as pervasive and formidable as ever Christianity was in the so-called ages of faith.

In the hundred years prior to Vatican II the
Catholic Church tackled the problem of minority
credibility by seeking to maintain a partially closed
society of its own, subsisting within the wider framework of western society but operating in some
respects against it: the much criticised 'ghetto Catholicism' of our childhood. Whatever the flaws of that
arrangement, it served as a 'plausibility structure'
in Berger's sense – though its effectiveness was per-

haps overestimated. But the fact is that the ghetto has gone, and almost certainly gone for good.

This does not mean that the looser, more open structure of contemporary Catholicism has altogether ceased to provide a distinctive, corporate and supportive framework for Christian belief. But in spite of the emphasis which has been placed on 'community' in the life of the Church in the years since Vatican II the Christian believer – at least in most of Western Europe – is a lonelier and more vulnerable figure than he was even thirty years ago; and that situation seems likely to persist.

Where social support for belief has been weakened other sources of validation take on relatively greater importance. The routine observance which safeguarded the faith of thousands in a formally Christian society will not meet the needs of the members of a cognitive minority. Christians who live as members of contemporary, post-Christian, western society, and who rightly want to be full members of that society, open to all that is good in it and in fruitful intellectual dialogue with it, can do so as Christians only if their own personal grasp of the unseen realities of the Christian faith is deep and firm enough to withstand the (often unconscious) social and psychological pressures which tend to erode the plausibility of those realities or render them irrelevant. A second-hand acceptance of Christian faith and practice, if it ever was enough, is so no longer. Each individual believer needs to make the realities of belief his own, to experience them *as* realities. This is a continuing, life-long process; and its instrument is personal prayer, informed by sound doctrine, tempered by experience of life and expressed in conduct.

Personal prayer does not mean only, or even mainly, private prayer, though private prayer is surely an essential element in the process. It means prayer which is not just formal or vocal but which involves conscious and continuing interior acts of attention and assent. In this sense, liturgical prayer is or should be personal prayer just as much as private or silent prayer is.

Exterior activity – social, political, domestic – can of course be a form of prayer: *laborare est orare* is an ancient Christian maxim. But by itself it is not enough. Only by adverting consciously and regularly to the source and object of his faith – that is by personal prayer – can the Christian in an unbelieving society keep his faith alive. Only by prayer can he build into the fabric of his daily life a pattern of personal experience and a habit of mind – in the Aristotelian sense of virtue as a 'habit' – which authenticates the unseen realities to which his faith is directed. And it is only from individual believers whose faith is authenticated – validated – in this way that the Church as a corporate entity can draw the credibility it needs in order to present the Gospel with conviction to non-believers and to remain a source of strength and reassurance to believers.

So far I have been making the narrow, and what some may think utilitarian, point that prayer is necessary in order to keep alive in ourselves and in the Church an awareness of the reality of the supernatural without which the faith will atrophy and be submerged in the prevailing secular worldview:

prayer, so to speak, as a corrective to spiritual defeatism.

Although I believe that this is a valid and important point to make, it also risks presenting prayer as a means to an end instead of what it really is, an end in itself from which all sorts of beneficial effects may flow. The end of prayer is worship – the recognition by the individual of the complete sovereignty of God. The beneficial effects are the consequences of that worship for the believer and for the community of believers.

This is difficult ground, where it is more than ever presumptuous to try to generalise. Clearly, prayer is not 'effective' in any measurable or consistent sense. Its results cannot be quantified or predicted. Much prayer seems sterile or goes apparently unanswered, leaving the one who prays empty or disheartened. People who pray do not, God knows, stop being sinners. They continue to give way to their passions, to act selfishly, foolishly, narrowmindedly, uncharitably or wickedly. Nevertheless, the attitudes and dispositions required in order to pray are good in themselves and recognisably conducive – in principle – to holiness.

For example, all prayer involves finding time for God and seeking to make oneself aware of him. This is the foundation of the spiritual life. All prayer involves surrendering, or trying to surrender, the whole of one's interior life to God – mind, heart and will. It thus generates an openness to what God wants and a disposition to try (not necessarily successfully, of course) to subordinate one's own will to his. All prayer involves forgiveness: you cannot pray and refuse to forgive. Hence it generates a disposition to tolerance, generosity and gentleness. All prayer involves an openness to truth and a disposition to seek it: there is no room for phoniness or self-deceit in a confrontation with God. All prayer generates a sense of perspective, in which quarrels, resentments and differences lose something of their cutting edge, and difficulties and sorrows loom a shade less crushingly. Thus reconciliation, understanding for another's point of view (however idiotic) and acceptance of one's own sufferings become easier. All prayer induces a disposition to gratitude, a disposition to humility, to see our successes as God's successes and not our own, and a sensitivity to the claims and concerns of one's neighbour. The prayer of praise, which constitutes so large a part of the official prayer of the Church, as well as inculcating gratitude and reverence, helps to counter the prevailing atmosphere of corrosive criticism and cynicism. All prayer involves interior stillness and silence, and hence provides an antidote to the incessant talkativeness which characterises so much secular (and religious) discourse.

One could lengthen the list, but it is perhaps long enough to make the point that, simply in terms of the dispositions it induces and irrespective of the generosity with which the Lord may respond, prayer is a potentially transforming force both for the individual believer and for the Church as a whole (which is composed of individual believers). I hope it is also enough to dispose of the thought that there is something inherently selfish about prayer or, alternatively, that to stress the primacy of prayer is to neglect the social dimension of Christianity, the Christian's responsibility for his neighbour, which has been so much to the fore since Vatican II. The truth is that prayer and conduct are inextricably interlinked and interact with one another. Just as misconduct is an obstacle to prayer, so prayer generates and overflows into self-giving love and beneficent action. Prayer is not an alternative to social or political concern but prompts, informs and tempers it. In the words of Archbishop William Temple: 'People are always thinking that conduct is supremely important, and that because prayer helps it, therefore prayer is good. That is true as far as it goes; still truer is it to say that worship is of supreme importance and conduct tests it. Conduct tests how much of yourself was in the worship you gave to God.'

Prayer, in short, is the heart of the matter. For prayer addresses what is unique in the Christian revelation and the Christian life, the unseen, personal, loving God on whom the Christian faith is posited. To neglect prayer is gradually to lose what distinguishes the Christian faith from a mere ethical or political system, to lose what distinguishes the institutional Church, with all its manifest faults, from other bureaucratic and social structures of human origin. More positively, one has only to compare the characteristics of the Church which we ourselves comprise – the Church in all our quarrelsomeness, wordiness, formalism, bureaucracy and worldliness – with the dispositions which I suggested above can be induced by prayer, to see the extent of the transformation which could be the result of shifting the emphasis of reform from structure to spirit.

This is the sense of my contention that prayer is crucial, not just to the Church's survival, but to what the Church is *for*. The Church exists, after all, to provide the visible, social, institutional framework within which people can meet and recognise the living God, and to be the community in which God manifests himself. In that capacity the Church, we know, is *semper reformanda:* but the value of any reform is to be measured strictly by the extent to which it promotes or detracts from the Church's central purpose. No other criterion is relevant.

Prayer is crucial to the central purpose because prayer opens the way to holiness, which is the presence of God made manifest in the human personality; and holiness is the touchstone of the Church's credibility. Without holiness, that spark of supernatural life which is kindled by prayer, the Church appears like a great country house from which the family has departed and which is maintained as a museum: vast, oppressive, nostalgic, decorative or repellent according to taste, and, in the last analysis, dead. This is the Church which is familiar to us from the writings of countless critics; the Church as people so often see it from the outside, and not by any means only from the outside; it is the Church as it appears to all of us in our moments of resentment, disillusionment or disbelief.

Making changes to the structure and outward appearance of the Church without prior regard to the quality of its spiritual life may give an illusion of reform, but it is an illusion only. True reform is a natural expression of spiritual vitality, not a substitute for it. Equally, however, when spiritual vitality is present, structural and organisational reform, however desirable, becomes less important. In the presence of holiness, defects of style and structure are secondary: the building has the heart of the matter in it. Those who discern holiness in the Church will forgive everything that is wrong with its organisation and behaviour and be drawn to follow where the Church points. Those who don't, won't.

One encouraging footnote. As a result of the Council, the Church has transformed its liturgy and made far reaching changes in its social and political attitudes. These are, on the whole, the changes on which public attention and controversy have focussed. But as well as the reform of the liturgy, there has been the reform of the Divine Office, revised by Pope Paul VI with the declared purpose of enabling it to become an instrument of meditative prayer not just for clergy and religious but for the laity as well. It was a reform which attracted relatively little attention at the time: perhaps in the long run, as the leaven of regular, meditative prayer works its way slowly through the Church, it may turn out to have been one of the most important.

2.

Dealing with difficulties

Edward Yarnold S J

It is remarkable how many words associated with difficulty in prayer begin with the letter D. Difficulties lead to despondency, depression, and disgust, though perhaps falling short of despair. They often take the form of distraction, dryness and darkness.

1. Distraction

Everybody who has ever tried to pray knows what distractions are. Distraction breeds distraction with the fecundity of flu germs multiplying in a mild winter. Distractions even have the ability to feed off themselves: when we catch ourselves following some fascinating line of distractions, and are just about to turn back to the Lord, the question comes into our mind, 'How did I get to that point?', and we spend the next five minutes retracing the series, like a chess-player replaying the moves of a game.

Sometimes distractions are our own fault. Prayer should normally begin with a few moments in which we seek to gather ourselves into stillness, but if we try to go straight into prayer from some experience that has sent images racing through our head or has set powerful emotions churning inside us perhaps all we can hope to accomplish in a period of prayer is to calm ourselves down. If we are generous in our intentions, we must choose a time of day for prayer when there will be a minimum of interference hindering the Holy Spirit from speaking in our hearts, so that stillness becomes our starting-point, and not the limit of our achievement.

All the same, however careful we are in trying to set up the optimum conditions, sometimes prayer will seem to be nothing but a fight against distraction. The important point here, as with the other kinds of difficulty, is to realise that the struggle itself is a form of prayer. Every time we turn our attention away from a distraction and back to God, we are performing an act of love of God.

Moreover, distractions may be only disturbances on the surface of a current of prayer that is flowing strongly underneath them. Although we all learn to pray by repeating forms of words, prayer is an activity which engages a far deeper level of our personalities than is required for even the attentive recitation of formulas. The essential nature of prayer is conveyed in the traditional definition: 'the raising up of the mind and heart to God.' Without this basic loving attention there is no prayer: our words may rise up, but our hearts remain below. Conversely, this loving attention may be present without any words or even without any articulated thoughts running through our heads. It may also continue underneath distraction. Indeed, it is possible that it may even contribute to distraction. For the God

towards whom this basic attention is directed tran-
scends all our ideas of him. Consequently our ima-
gination, finding nothing to do, naturally ranges far
and wide. It was St Teresa's advice that, when the
understanding wandered, we should not try to drag
it back by force, but simply laugh at it.

2. Dryness

Unlike distractions, which are the common experience of everyone who prays, the second difficulty,
dryness, is experienced mainly by those who attempt
what is traditionally called mental prayer, i.e. prayer
which does not rely upon the recitation of composed
prayers. By dryness I mean a state in which,
although we are not distracted, we seem to be aware
of little other than the effort to pray, so that a minute
of this laborious emptiness seems to last half an
hour.

The reason for this, and for the darkness which
we shall consider next, may be simple tiredness. Dry
prayer may take the form of a constant struggle
against sleep. In that case it can be valuable to take
up an uncomfortable position, kneeling, for example,
or standing, rather than sitting, or even (in private)
praying with outstretched arms, as people do by the
grotto at Lourdes. In this way, the very physical
unease can become part of our prayer; the body
prays along with the mind and the heart.

The vital principle in dryness is not to give up.
We will naturally feel that it would be better to
spend the time more productively, say in reading the
Bible or a spiritual book, or in repeating vocal

prayers. But this may be a temptation. One can imagine Screwtape writing about it to his nephew. 'My dear Wormwood, If you see your client trying to achieve a deeper level of prayer, give him a dose of drudgery and drowsiness (two more Ds!), and then suggest that instead of such an unprofitable exercise, he would do much better to spend the time reading the Bible or reading about prayer.' It was Jean-Pierre de Caussade's advice that at prayer we should be prepared to be like a statue if that was God's wish, glorifying him at least by our faithful presence. Although such an attitude could result from a resigned despair, it can also express a deep trust in the fidelity of God.

3. Darkness

The third difficulty, darkness, like the second, is one recognisable in mental rather than in vocal prayer. Darkness can take a variety of forms. It can be felt as a sense of boredom, futility, or sometimes repulsion with regard to prayer. It can even be experienced as a fear that we no longer believe (though the particular anguish that this fear can cause suggests that it is not unbelief that we are experiencing).

One form of the experience was described by the anonymous medieval English mystic as a 'cloud of unknowing'. 'You find nothing but a darkness, and so to speak a cloud of unknowing – you do not understand it, except that you feel in your will a naked intent towards God. This darkness and this cloud . . . hinder you, so that you neither see him clearly by the light of understanding in your reason, nor feel him in sweetness and love in your affection' (*Cloud of Unknowing*, ch. 3).

Just as the effort to pray in spite of distraction and dryness is itself prayer, the same is true of prayer in darkness. When prayer is easy, sweet and full of readily recognisable consolation we will pray, not only for God's sake, but also for what we get out of it. But when God sends us darkness and other forms of difficulty in prayer he is inviting us to pray simply because we trust him, because we cling to the fact that it is right to pray. This prayer, accordingly, has been described as the Prayer of Faith.

But we can go further than this. It is not just that the effort to pray is prayer in spite of the darkness; the darkness may be itself prayer, and indeed the heart of all prayer. What we are experiencing is not prayer expressed in words or thoughts or feelings, but the bare essence of prayer, the naked intent towards God.

In darkness, as in distraction and dryness, the fundamental rule is not to give up, nor to go back to a less deep and demanding form of prayer. But it is often difficult to get people to accept this advice. It regularly happens that someone who becomes aware of this experience for the first time cannot recognise it for what it is, but is convinced that it is due to some shortcoming on their part.

It is therefore important to identify this darkness. However, the reason why we try to do this is not the desire to be able to congratulate ourselves on our progress, for any form of prayer, being a supernatural activity, is wholly a gift of God; the ability to pray without words is not in itself a greater mark of God's love than the ability to pray vocally. The reason for trying to identify this darkness is simply the need to react to it in the right way: to persevere rather than shopping around for methods of prayer that promise more palpable results, or abandoning mental prayer altogether.

There are, then, various signs which help us to recognise this darkness.

The first sign is that there are none of the obvious natural reasons for the darkness. Like dryness, there can be natural darkness due to tiredness or illness. Again, like distractions, darkness may be due to the engagement of our minds with the images and concerns of our everyday life. If that is the case, we must do what we can to get out of natural darkness by disposing ourselves properly for prayer. We cannot advance in prayer unless we want to; and if we want to, we must be prepared to pay the price of the discipline of doing all we can to come to prayer with minds that are still, but alert and attuned to God. When the great writers on prayer insist that progress is impossible without mortification, this self-discipline is perhaps one of the things they have in mind.

The second sign of supernatural darkness is that we are not aware of a persistent avoidance of God's will. This is not to say that only saints can experience a darkness that is real prayer: such prayer exists to make sinners less unholy, as well as to make saints holier. But if we refuse to admit even to ourselves that God may be making a particular demand upon us, there can hardly exist that openness of spirit which prayer requires. All the same, it may be possible for a person who is resisting God's will to pray at depth, provided that they acknowledge to themselves and to God that they are too afraid or too ungenerous to say Yes. One can look God in the eyes in prayer and say, 'Lord, I daren't'. It is the shifty refusal to acknowledge the demands of that gaze that limits us to the fringes of prayer.

A third criterion for recognising this darkness is the presence of a deep desire for prayer. Some writers prefer to speak of the presence of a deep desire for God; but this desire for God often takes the form of a felt need for prayer.

A fourth sign by which we can recognise this darkness is the contrast between the readiness with which we think about God and experience his presence outside the time of formal prayer and the sensation that, as soon as we enter into formal prayer, a fog decends so that thought about God is impossible.

There is a fifth criterion, which is the most important of all, the criterion of the fruit tree: 'You will know them by their fruits ... A sound tree cannot bear evil fruit, nor can a bad tree bear good fruit' (Matthew 7: 16, 18). If we can honestly recognise in our lives a growing generosity in our following of Christ our prayer cannot be self-delusion.

We cannot, then, simply link the three Ds which are the names of difficulties in prayer with a fourth D, the Devil. At least the difficulties are a challenge to a more faithful and generous prayer. At best, a difficulty may be itself prayer, in which the Source of all Light shines upon us with what St John of the Cross called a 'ray of darkness'.

The advice to be given is always the same. First, we must remove as far as we can the obstacles we are placing in the way of our prayer. Secondly, we must not lose heart, but persevere. Thirdly, it is a valuable help to read one of the classical works on prayer or a modern exposition of them. Fourthly, the advice of a spiritual guide is almost indispensable. Lastly, if anyone does not recognise his own experiences in this description of difficulties, he need not worry. There are many jewels in God's treasure-chest. Each must pray in the way God's grace enables him to pray, without pining for other forms of prayer.

3.

Examination of conscience

Margaret Hebblethwaite

Many of us think we have grown out of examining
our consciences. What we have really grown out of
is a childish way of self-examination, without yet
growing into a more adult approach. We are haunted
by those awful lists at the back of prayer books, with
different sins for men and for women – Have I been
faithful to the morning offering? Have I shown
disrespect for the Blessed Virgin Mary? Have I
subscribed to Catholic newspapers and periodicals?
Have I observed modesty in dress?

None of us ever actually achieves such a thing as
a wholly mature conscience. The very fact of sin
means that we never fully arrive at the state of seeing
everything in its true perspective. But making a
place, every so often, for examination of conscience
in our lives means that we have a chance of some
slight moves towards maturity. The examination
should not itself reinforce immaturity by limiting
itself to going down the same inadequate checklist
in the same way over and over again, thus reassuring
ourselves ever more firmly that our greatest sins are
some pious trifles while the great glaring beams of
what is really wrong in our lives become more and

more invisible to our eyes. Any honest examination must work within the bounds of an honest question – not, 'What do I think the Church is telling me I ought to think is wrong with my life?', but, 'What do I really think is wrong with my life?'

One of the reasons (of course not the only reason) why so many people do not use the sacrament of reconciliation is because they do not know how to answer that question. They do not know what to say in confession. They shy off examination of conscience because they do not know any productive or illuminating ways of approaching it and yet they feel a genuine Christian need to acknowledge that they are sinners. They know the inner sense of sin that has been described by the Oxford Dominican, Simon Tugwell, as 'a profound conviction that I am in the way', but they are uncertain how to apply that in any specific ways to the raw material of their lives. As we move through Lent and each face at least a fleeting consideration of what to do about our 'Easter duties' we may like to set aside some time for examination of conscience, whether or not we would also like to receive absolution for our sins in the sacrament of reconciliation.

The starting point for examination of conscience is to realise that it is an act of prayer, and only makes sense if it is approached with a sense of God's presence. As we bring ourselves before God we become conscious of the great gap between God's holiness and our tangledness. We become conscious that there are blocks between us and our God. We want to acknowledge them as fully as we can, and ask God's help in moving them, and we do this in the faith that no sin is too big for God's free and happy forgiveness. That is the context that makes examination of conscience not psychoanalysis but prayer. It is the context of a relationship with someone who loves us, and whom we want to love more freely.

Having begun our examination by placing ourselves honestly, vulnerably and trustingly in God's presence, we can then proceed in one of three different ways. First, we can see what naturally arises from our own lives – looking to see 'what is on our conscience'. Or secondly, we can more systematically measure ourselves against some questions: it does not have to be a list at the back of a prayer book or the ten commandments, though those two guides may be the first that spring to mind. Or thirdly, we can use Scripture: this gives us an external measure for seeing what reflections arise when we place our own lives under the lamp of biblical teaching.

Starting from our own life

Ignatius of Loyola's 'General Examen' is the classic summary of the examination that starts from our own life. It is often called an 'examen of consciousness' rather than an 'examen of conscience' in the narrow sense, because it looks for all the ways in which God has been touching our lives, and how we have responded or failed to respond: sin emerges as part of the total picture rather than as a series of isolated acts. It is often recommended as a quarter-of-an-hour's reflection at the end of the day; but it can be done for any stretch of our lives – the last year, the time since our last confession, or our life up till now.

Ignatius suggests five points, which will probably all play a part if we let our prayer unfold naturally. First, we start with thanking God for what he has done for us. (That puts sin in the right context of unresponsiveness to God's gifts.) Secondly, we realise that knowledge of our sins is a grace, and so we ask for that grace. (After all, we spend so much time avoiding this particular grace that we may need to turn round consciously and open ourselves to it.) Thirdly, we recall the events and experiences of our lives, noticing how our changing feelings indicate the areas of sin. Fourthly, we say that we are sorry. And fifthly we ask for God's help to change and grow. ('Confession without change is a game,' said Thomas A. Harris in *I'm OK – You're OK*.)

The tone of this approach is not so much to look for transgressions of rules as to become aware of the deeper satisfactions or dissatisfactions that reflect the presence or absence of the Spirit. What we find we most want to thank God for may not be the new clothes we have just splashed out on but something as simple as having had the chance to say something kind to someone in need. What we feel most uneasy about before God in prayer may turn out not to be our financial worries but the fact that we have made exaggerated criticisms of someone of whom we are jealous.

What we are looking for is how we have been in or out of tune with the invitation to live our lives with and for God, and so we pay more attention to our moods than to details of external behaviour.

Over-scrupulous nit-picking can lead to a sense of
scratching where it does not really itch but where
we think perhaps it ought to and where, if we scratch
hard enough, perhaps it will. But attention to the
subtle movements of our feelings can reveal something about our fundamental option. As we become
aware of what makes us miserable and what makes
us happy we learn about the values that are guiding
our lives, and we can move from following what we
think we want (perhaps a more prestigious job) to
what we most deeply desire (the love and service of
God). And so we are led in a natural progression
to talk to God honestly about how we are and to ask
his mercy and help in the problematic and sinful
parts of our lives. But it is not only this direct talking
to God that is the prayer: the whole process of
bringing our lives before God is all prayer. This
form of examination of conscience may well throw
up matter that we would like to bring before God
in confession, but any such sins should emerge in
context – the context of our life as a whole, and the
context of response to God's grace.

Starting from questions

Sometimes it is helpful to gain more perspective
on our lives by starting from a point outside ourselves, so that we are putting questions to ourselves
rather than just waiting for what floats up to the
surface. In addition to the ten commandments Ignatius suggests we can use the measure of the seven
capital sins, the three powers of the soul, and the
five senses of the body.

The seven capital sins are pride, covetousness, lust, anger, gluttony, envy and sloth. That may sound rather melodramatic, largely because the words themselves are rather archaic, but we can turn them into questions that make sense to us, and that may draw our attention to forgotten areas. What am I proud about? What are my ambitions? What does sex mean for me? Have I shown anger and if so was it constructive? Have I suppressed anger in any areas of my life, and if so is it doing damage? How dependent am I on eating and drinking? Have I got professional jealousies, or jealousies in relationships? What am I lazy about? We gain another dimension if, as Ignatius suggests, we turn our minds to the corresponding positive qualities: what would humility mean in my life? And generosity? And so on.

The three powers of the soul are memory, understanding and will. It is amazing what can be thrown up if we think about sin in these areas. A sin of memory could be to pay too little attention to the moments of special joy and insight that I have been given: remembering what led me to marry can refocus me on loving my partner; remembering the joy of a conversion experience can make me realise how much I take God for granted when I could be constantly praising him. We can also sin in our memories by editing out the human misery that passes on the edge of our lives – the photos of starving children in charity advertisements; the threats to world peace that I prefer not to think about; the letter I should have written long ago to someone who is longing to hear from me. We can sin in our understanding by having closed and prejudiced minds; we can sin in our will by failing to do the things we know we ought to do and mean to do one day but have never got round to.

Sinning with our five senses is largely a matter of insensitivity and unresponsiveness. Do I only look up to the sky to see whether to take an umbrella, or do I live in constant appreciation of the stunning skyscapes that God provides for me every day? When I touch others am I saying 'I care for you'? And so on.

There are many other ways of adapting this approach to examination of conscience, so that stagnation should never set in. We can go through sins of thought, word, deed and omission. We can consider sins against God, against others, and against ourselves. We can use the Beatitudes: What would it mean for me to be poor in spirit? Am I gentle? Do I let myself mourn? Do I hunger and thirst for justice? To whom have I been merciful? Is my heart set on the pure, single-minded search for God? How can I be a peacemaker? What could it mean for me to be persecuted in the cause of right?

Another excellent guide is the list of fruits of the Holy Spirit, based on Galatians 5:22. Does my life show the fruits of love? joy? peace? patience? kindness? goodness? faithfulness? gentleness? self-control? In which do I most fall short?

Starting from Scripture

The approach from Scripture is at the same time the most oblique and, in the end, the most transforming. The New Rite of Penance has introduced into confession a reading from Scripture 'whenever there is an opportunity'. If there is not time for it the Scripture reading 'may be done as part of the preparation for the sacrament'. Considering how rarely time is found for this during the sacrament itself it is a very good idea to make sure that we always use Scripture in our preparation and let it feed into our examination of conscience.

There is scarcely a passage in the whole Bible, let alone in the New Testament, that cannot be used for this purpose, to show up some of our sins. For example, if I pray over Passion Sunday's gospel of the entry into Jerusalem I might become aware of how difficult I would find it to herald Jesus with that kind of abandoned celebration: I might become conscious that I am too reserved, or too fearful, or too sceptical, or too traditionalist, to let myself give way to such jubilant praise of Christ. Or I might be struck by Jesus's courage in entering the city where he knew he was to face death: I might wonder when I had shown courage in my own life, and whether I would have been brave enough to follow him in those last days of crisis. I might think about the fickleness of the crowd, who one day were meeting Jesus with cries of welcome and so soon afterwards were to cry out 'Crucify him': Do I show the same tendency to 'go with the crowd' rather than act out of personal conviction? Or again, it might be the aspect of the poor king, riding on a colt, that draws my attention: I might contrast my tendency to look up to the rich and powerful with the Christian invitation to find Jesus among the poor and simple. Whatever way the text challenges me I am unlikely to find myself as the spontaneously perfect disciple, unless I am cheating.

Whichever mode of examination of conscience we use it will not reveal much unless we approach it in a truly prayerful way. We are so used to self-justification and self-protection that we need to trust in God's unconditional love for us before we dare to admit that we have done wrong or need to change. We need reverence and awe on the one hand, confidence in God's forgiveness on the other. We need to have a minimal wanting to want to do his will. But we also need an awareness of how weak and useless we are without his help. We ask for the Lord's light in knowing ourselves, just as we ask for his strength in moving towards closer discipleship. They are precious moments when we can stand before God (in prayer, or in the sacrament) as we really are, without pretence, and know that our shared acknowledgment of our faults is a cause of intimacy and a new bond of love.

4.

Contemplative reading

Felicitas Corrigan OSB

The Vatican Council has swept away the nonsense which spoke of contemplation as if it were an extraordinary grace, the perquisite of a select coterie: it is God's gift to every Christian soul in baptism. 'It is not true,' St Gregory the Great assured his congregation, in his ninth homily on the gospels, 'that the grace of contemplation is given to the highest and not to the lowest. There is no state of life of the faithful from which it is excluded. Anyone who keeps his heart within may be illumined by the light of contemplation.' The phrase, 'to keep and return to one's heart or inner self' is for St Gregory a kind of signature tune.

For example, he turns the parable of the talents upside down. According to the gospels, our Lord as he sat on the Mount of Olives told his disciples how a man going on a journey entrusted his property to his servants: to one he gave five talents; to another, two; to a third, one. Plain as a pikestaff. But is it? The five talents, St Gregory says, are the five senses; the two, intellect and will; the one talent is the greatest of all: '*Intellectus* and nothing else whatever is designated by the one talent.' Obviously there

must be a profound difference between the *intellectus*
comprised in the two talents and that of one. The
first is the faculty of reasoning and understanding,
a matter of human brain power. The other, the
supreme gift, is the gift of spiritual understanding,
a very different proposition. As so often with the
fathers, the context supplies what no dictionary does.
'We see daily in holy Church,' he tells the packed
crowd gathered to listen to him in the Lateran
Basilica, 'that very many manage external duties yet
are led to *intellectus mysticus*, and are gifted greatly
with inward understanding.' With him, mystical
understanding and contemplation are interchange-
able terms.

In Gregory's most famous book, *Pastoral Care*,
which King Alfred translated in the ninth century
under the title *Shepherd's Book* – one that is still
used and useful in our own – 'ignorance of the light
of heavenly contemplation' (1,2) at once disqualifies
any candidate for the priesthood. Yet this one talent
which is death to hide is, with far too many Christians, lodged useless. More is the pity because in
one sense it is the easiest and most profitable of all
to trade with. 'The Spirit himself bears witness to
our spirit that we are the children of God' (Romans
8:16), and that Spirit who searches everything, even
the depths of God, helps us in our weakness (cf. 1
Corinthians 2:10).

If the point has been laboured it is because contemplation is the beginning and end of *lectio divina*.
The root of the word 'contemplation' means simply
to gaze steadily at something. You see people standing rapt before a beautiful picture or lovely land-

scape, and the longer they look, the more they see. This stillness, this steady gaze of concentration is the root of all *lectio:* 'Be still and see that I am God.'

The term *lectio divina* – reading from the Sacred Books – is derived from monastic usage. 'What page or what utterance of the divinely-inspired books of the Old and New Testaments,' St Benedict asks in the Epilogue to his Rule, 'is not a most unerring rule of human life? Or what book of the holy Catholic fathers does not loudly proclaim how we may come by a straight course to our Creator?' That puts it in a nutshell. To the early fathers there is only one book, the Bible: around it, their thought, conduct, whole lives revolve.

Lectio is not reading 'a spiritual book', nor is it scientific scriptural exegesis; it is not even prayer in its accepted sense. What is it then? St Benedict places it in Chapter 48 of the Rule, 'On the daily manual labour.' 'Idleness is the enemy of the soul. The brethren therefore must be occupied at certain hours in manual labour, and again at other hours *in lectione divina.*' On Sundays however *lectioni vacent omnes* – all should devote the time to reading.

The verb *vacent* is interesting in the context: it denotes leisure, taking a little holiday (our word 'vacation'), being empty and receptive. There will be no pathological symptoms of any kind: we shall not stop to ask ourselves, 'Am I in the purgative, illuminative or unitive way?' We shall simply let the tension in the office yesterday or the menu for tomorrow's dinner go hang, select our book or passage of the Old or New Testament as St Benedict prescribes and, for at least a quarter of an hour,

allow the Holy Spirit to draw us, naked and unclutt-
ered, into the orbit of God. To quote St Gregory's
Moralia, 'The voice of God is heard when, with
minds at ease, we rest from the bustle of this world
and ponder the divine precepts in the deep silence
of the mind.'

The reading chosen will depend on one's particular bent: there can be no regimentation. As Nistero,
the desert father, pointed out: 'Abraham was hos-
pitable and God was with him; Elijah loved quiet
and God was with him; David was humble and God
was with him. What therefore you find your soul
desires in following God, that do, and keep your
heart.'

Hosea and the minor prophets might strike the
right note for beginners: 'I will allure her, and bring
her into the wilderness, and speak tenderly to her'
(Hosea 2:14). The essential is to read very slowly,
possibly aloud, possibly with repetition. Do as Bede
tells us Caedmon did: chew the cud of God's word,
extract all the nourishment you can, take and eat
this manna, the bread from heaven, which is God's
Word exactly as the Holy Eucharist is that Word
made flesh.

For myself, as Lenten reading I should choose
just three psalms: 90 (*Qui habitat*), 129 (*De profundis*), and 21 (*Deus, Deus meus*). Nothing draws us
so powerfully into the mind of Christ himself as the
psalms. They were his own prayer book, and in
them he worships, rejoices, suffers for and in his
brethren, and speaks to his Father, now as Head,
now as Body; occasionally we overhear a mysterious
dialogue between the two.

Texts from Psalm 90 run throughout the Lenten liturgy, like the theme of a great symphony. Have you noticed there are three voices speaking? Hidden with Christ in God, I utter the battle-cry of my Lenten observance in the first two verses. In response, the Church, Christ's Bride, gives assurance and encouragement from verses 3 to 13. The final three verses are the promise of the Father to his Son about to enter on the *via dolorosa,* and to each one of us: after death, the glory of resurrection.

Psalm 129, *De profundis,* is restricted all too often to prayer for the dead, but that is not the mind of the Church. It is used at Christmas Vespers, and, like all God's word, has layer upon layer of mystery and meaning. Try to enter into it on Maundy Thursday night – that terrible experience of our Lord when, after the agony in Gethsemane, he spent the night with the soldiery, and in his Father's sight became sin for our sake. *De profundis* – the Nothing calls upon the All. And always, the promise of the Father, of life out of death.

Psalm 21 is Messianic in the strictest sense: the Son of God is afraid and horror-stricken at the chastisement for sin that is to rob him of life in the full flower of his manhood. We must not stop there: he is in agony in his members until the end of time, and it may be that in our own woe under trial and affliction we shall find its perfect expression in his cry. But from verse 23 onwards, what joy, what triumph, what fruit, what future glory! These things the Lord will do, Blessed be God.

5.

In the midst of life

Martha Skinnider

A life of prayer has traditionally been associated with religious, who were protected by withdrawal from the 'world' and a rule of silence. Today, in the light of Vatican II, it is recognised more fully that God is present in this world and can be found there. Nor is a life of prayer any longer seen as the preserve of clergy and religious: there is a real desire among lay people to share it. There is, therefore, a growing demand from lay men and women for the help of conferences, retreats, and days of recollection as well as for regular spiritual direction.

Inevitably this demand can be met only for a small number. If the opportunity to live a life of prayer is not to be denied to the majority of the laity then a simpler means of help and support for growth in prayer must be found.

If prayer is seen as basically being open to God then we do not have far to look. We find God in his world. He is within us and in our lives. Growth in prayer depends upon becoming aware of him there.

A simple pattern of the growth of this awareness can be found in St Luke's account of the journey to Emmaus. Two despondent men are walking along the road. A stranger joins them and then walks along with them. He listens to where they are at in their lives – to their experience. He throws onto that experience the light of the scriptures. As they listen, their awareness of their situation begins to change. They respond in their invitation to the stranger to stay with them. In the breaking of bread, an action taking place in their life experience, they find that they have not lost Jesus, that he is still with them in a more powerful way than before. After this discovery their lives can never be the same – they are changed.

This pattern I have found helpful, living in one of Glasgow's peripheral housing schemes. We are labelled by bureaucracy as an area of Multiple Deprivation. Most of the industries in which our people worked have disappeared: far from the city, with few facilities, this is not a place where many people would want to live.

We may not have a deep knowledge of Scripture, or an ease with books; we could find difficulty in affording conferences and retreats; but there is one thing in which we have a great richness and that is in life experience. Those who left the close-knit inner-city communities in the early 1950s to build up a new community without even basic facilities had spent their earlier years in the slums of Glasgow during the depression and war years. They did build up a real community in a housing wilderness and now have to watch it deteriorate in the recession. Those who came here as children and shared in the development of the community now find themselves redundant, and watch their children leave school without hope of real employment.

Despite our problems, we are a very friendly, accepting community. We talk easily to each other whether we are friends, acquaintances or strangers who meet 'on the road'. The weather may be our starting point but sharing of experiences can be quickly reached. To be an Emmaus companion to someone wishing to grow in prayer comes naturally in this community.

I find myself listening to where people are at in their lives, as we meet in residents' groups, or parish groups, as I come along the road, or as I shop. It is simple to move from this to a more formal setting – a meeting with an individual in her home or mine. As I listen to problems or difficulties in life I suggest that we try to find where God is in the experience. When this suggestion is accepted, the journey begins.

We move first of all to establishing that interior stillness and silence which enables us to find God within us, helped by simple stillness exercises from Fr Anthony de Mello's book *Sadhana: A Way to God*. This silence must be found in the midst of exterior noise, as houses are small, sound-proofing minimal, and tenement living is not conducive to a quiet atmosphere; and it must be found in the midst of family life. When the beginner has experienced this stillness, I encourage her to make a commitment to set aside a specific time each day for prayer – even fifteen minutes is sufficient – and for a weekly meeting with me of about an hour. It is at this stage that we begin to travel on the road.

We look back over our lives, finding where God has been in our life experience. Reliving and feeling again particularly joyful memories can be a springboard for this. At the same time we begin to pray each day using Scripture. Any of the many passages speaking of God's loving and fatherly care of the individual enlighten our remembering, and show us that our life has not only a history but a faith history. Knowledge of Scripture is not necessary for the passages to speak to us in our lives. We have little temptation to intellectualise the reading of Scripture. We let it speak to our hearts and lives.

Gradually the prayer begins to move, as we take two or three passages for prayer each week. The companion is at all times a listener – listening carefully to the report of what has happened each week in life and in prayer. She listens for the signs of the prayer moving on from the joy of knowing the Father's love and the realisation of what he has done for us to a consideration of what our response to that love has been.

Moving on to this stage, the companion has now to accompany someone as they look in the light of Scripture at their failure to respond to God's love. This can be a time when much support is needed as we face our true sinfulness, as distinct from the sinful acts we commit. But it is being faced in the recent experience of God's loving care, and Scripture will now highlight his loving forgivness. Again for several weeks the companion listens until the message comes over from the beginner that she realises with joy that God loves her as she is – a sinner, and only he can help her to change.

With this realisation the prayer normally moves to a desire to respond to God for all he has done for us. Passages from the New Testament on God's call;

passages showing Jesus and his apostles at work;
passages speaking of the way Jesus's followers
should live – all can help us to be aware where God
is asking for growth and response.

At this point the formal walking together comes
to an end. But if the companion has been true to her
role, this is the beginning of a real life of prayer. A
true companion is one who supports and facilitates
the growing awareness of God in daily life, but does
not interfere in God's dealing with the beginner.
Therefore at the end of the formal walking together,
the companion bows out leaving the beginner not
alone, but with God, in the awareness she has of
God in her life – an awareness that deepens as life
goes on. An awareness, also, that calls for a continual
response.

It is in this continued response that growth takes
place. Although the initial journey has concentrated
on the individual and her relationship with God, it
has taken place in the midst of life. There has been
no danger of the prayer being isolated from relationships with others, or from events in the local community or even world events. The basic change
wrought is a change of attitude to ourselves as of
value, loved by God, and therefore an acceptance of
others as similarly valued. It is from this stance that
we respond to God as we meet him in our family,
in our friends, in everyone who comes our way,
whether they think like us or not. It is from this
stance that we respond to him as we meet him in
the needs of our own immediate community or the
needs of the wider world.

The pattern for this prayer experience in the

midst of life comes not from any modern master of spirituality but from Ignatius of Loyola, who lived in the first half of the sixteenth century. Ignatius intended that his full *Spiritual Exercises* could be given in two ways, either by withdrawal from everyday life for thirty days, or in the midst of life. Those following the second way continued with their daily routine but made a commitment to set aside a certain time each day for prayer and for a regular meeting with their director to give an account of the prayer. Ignatius stressed the non-directive role of the one who gives the *Exercises* '. . . as a balance at equilibrium . . . (he) should permit the Creator to deal directly with the creature and the creature directly with his Creator and Lord.'

Ignatius did not see the *Exercises* in daily life as an inferior way of making them but rather as an alternative way – widening their availability. Moreover, he did not see the giving of the *Exercises* as something confined to religious or clergy. He intended that those who followed the full *Exercises*, lay people, religious or clergy, would be able to accompany others through them.

Several people with whom I began the shorter prayer journey have committed themselves to the longer, more demanding *Spiritual Exercises* and completed them in six to nine months.

In the joy of the experience they want to share with others the gift which has been given them, and some desire to accompany others on the shorter prayer journey. This support and help coming from within the local community makes available to a much wider group the opportunity to grow in a life of prayer. We are learning, as Bernard of Clairvaux says, that it is essential, for our spiritual growth, 'to drink from our own wells'.

6.

God in all things

Gerard W. Hughes SJ

Imagine yourself going to visit the person whom you know best and love most. You enter the house using your own key and give a shout to announce your arrival. There is silence. You go into the front room. The beloved is sitting at a table, ignores your presence, and continues to scribble notes from an open book, with other volumes piled high on each side. You glance at a few of the titles: *How to Cultivate a Loving Friendship, The Art of Conversation, Healing Life's Hurts, Fighting Loneliness, The Layperson's Guide to Spirituality, A Compendium of Theology*. In response to your, 'What on earth's the matter with you: put that rubbish away,' your beloved looks up in terror, stands, bows low and then addresses you formally with one, or perhaps a selection of the following titles, 'Mother, Father, Superior, Prime Minister, Headmaster, Officer, Headmistress, Your Holiness,' and then launches into a speech of self-recrimination for past failings and expresses a determination never ever to behave so heinously again, ending with an 'Amen' before returning to the books and the scribbling. You stand benumbed for a few moments before going to the telephone and phoning the doctor.

This story describes most of us most of the time in our attitude towards God, our guest, who 'Watched my bones take shape when I was being formed in secret, knitted together in the limbo of the womb' (Psalm 138) and who, 'before the world was made, chose us in Christ to live through love in his presence' (Ephesians 1:4), in Christ, 'through whom and for whom all things were created, all things in heaven and on earth everything visible and everything invisible' (Colossians 1:15–16). God, in Christ, makes his home in us (John 14:23) and he is, in St Augustine's words, *'Intimior intimo meo,'* 'Closer to me than I to myself.' All things are his: his imperishable spirit is in everything. He loves us, not because we are good, or virtuous, or beautiful, well-integrated, meaningful persons, but because we are his creation, and his love is stronger than death, so that nothing can overcome the power of that love, which will remain when the mountains have crumbled and the hills departed (cf. Isaiah 54:10).

He is present in every experience of our lives, in the dark moments as well as in the light, sharing our sorrows as well as our joys. Yes, he is also present in our sins, for 'he became sin for us' (2 Corinthians 5:21) and he answers our sins with his love. 'One of the soldiers pierced his side with a lance; and immediately there came out blood and water' (John 19:34) 'for the life of the world' (John 6:51). He comes into our house not to punish but to heal: not to condemn, but to save. 'He overlooks men's sins so that they can repent' (Wisdom 11:23).

This loving presence permeates every particle of the universe, every recess of our minds and hearts.

'If I climb the heavens, you are there; there, too, if I lie in Sheol. If I flew to .the point of sunrise, or westward across the sea, your hand would still be guiding me, your right hand holding me. If I asked the darkness to cover me, and the light to become night around me, that darkness would not be dark to you, night would be as light as day' (Psalm 138).

Since God is in all things, there is no thing, no event, no inner experience, no thought or emotion, no evil we have done or evil done to us in which we cannot find him, in which he is not communicating his life and love to us. Prayer is acknowledging his presence. There is nothing in our experience which cannot become the subject of our prayer. Every event can become an encounter with him.

In the imaginary story with which I began, your presence was never acknowledged, because you were mistaken for your friend's parents, or some other authority figure: you were not acknowledged as you. Your friend's fears, anxieties and misgivings arising from past experience were so projected on to you that you were not recognised. This is what we do with God. We project images on to him, an amalgam of past influences, ideas and instructions, and approach and address him accordingly. 'The supreme Spirit who alone exists of himself and is infinite in all perfection' is not the kind of person with whom we are likely to enjoy a friendly chat or a bit of a laugh. Nor are we likely to feel relaxed with a God who has sown a minefield in this vale of tears with mines of two kinds: those who can injure and maim, but not kill, and are called 'venial mines', and others which can blow up your immortal

soul and are called 'mortal mines'. Our anxiety is
not lessened by the further information that in his
infinite mercy he has entrusted a map of the mine-
fields to the magisterium, who can tell us both where
the mines are and also how near we may go without
actually detonating them. Such a God is not the kind
of person we want to have around too often, for it
would be like having a well armed, trigger-happy,
grenade-jangling and very touchy terrorist as a constant escort.

We may find that we are too busy to pray or that,
when we do try, it is as though our minds explode
and fragment into innumerable pieces, leaving us
sore with some jagged memories and exhausted with
the effort of trying to raise what we thought was
our mind and heart to God, but which turns out to
be an inner vacuum. The reason may be that deep
in our consciousness is a disinclination to come too
near to God, or rather to our inherited image of
God.

'Be still and know that I am God.' Nothing so
hides the face of God as our own distorted images
of him. God is known by God alone. 'You have only
one teacher, the Christ' (Matthew 23:10). Let him
teach you in the only way he can, namely through
your own experience of life, for there is no other
way of knowing him. In prayer, heart speaks to
heart. Let him speak to your heart first of all, and
answer him first from your heart: otherwise we are
like the friend in the story who was so busy learning
the theory of friendship that there was no time for
you. We can be so preoccupied with clarifying our
ideas about God that we ignore his presence.

'He overlooks our sins', Wisdom says, 'so that we can repent,' so do not allow a sense of guilt to prevent you from turning to him. The Prodigal Son was full of guilt and had his repentance speech prepared: 'Father, I have sinned against heaven and against you.' But the father in the parable, who is God now holding us in being, apparently ignores this confession of guilt, embraces and kisses his son, clothes him in a robe, gives a ring for his finger and sandals for his feet and orders a celebration. It is only when we can begin to glimpse and accept the unconditional love of God that we can begin to know what we have missed and destroyed in ourselves and others – in other words, begin to repent.

If you cannot face long periods of prayer, practise spasmodic, split-second prayer. For example, you see someone or something beautiful: know that God is enjoying that experience of beauty within you. The writer of the prophecy of Daniel prayed in this way. Everything he experienced, sun, moon, stars, clouds, lightning, wind, showers, dew, fire, heat, ice, snow, sleet, frost and cold, mountains and hills, seas and rivers, beasts wild and tame, the fish of the sea (Daniel 3), became for him a source of prayer. He let the experience of all things flow through him and his sense experience became a litany of praise. We can do the same when we look at nature, at the features of human faces, at the light in people's eyes, when we experience the charm, goodness, gentleness, compassion and generosity of others. We share our delight with him and then we want to praise and thank him not because we ought to, but because we cannot help doing so.

But what of the darkness of life, the starving of this world, those dying in agony from disease, others from torture or violence? What of the terrors that lurk in the recesses of our minds, of the fear that hangs over us all, the fear of nuclear holocaust? We must pray these especially.

God is present in all our fears and terrors, weeping in our broken hearts. 'Do not be afraid' is his continual refrain in the Old Testament and in Christ. Christ is the image of the God we cannot see. In Christ's Passion God enters our darkness and despair. The powers of destruction hurl themselves at him. He absorbs the hatred and violence, giving in return the blood and water of his heart in which 'all things are reconciled through him and for him, everything in heaven and everything on earth, when he made peace by his death on the cross' (Colossians 1:20).

God, in Christ, has overcome all the powers of destruction. Jesus is Lord of all creation, of all ages, of all times. We must let him into our fears and crises, our disbelief and despair. All we have to do is to show it to him. He does not need our words, our theories, nor do we need to have done courses in philosophy and theology with special studies in the Problem of Evil before we approach him.

When we show him our pain, he will begin to teach us, showing us the root of it. Our hurt may spring from frustration that our attempts to build up the security of our own kingdom of wealth, success and self-importance are being thwarted. We begin to see the thwarting as a kindness, for our kingdom is a prison, a tomb, and he is breaking down its walls. We may still feel a residual pain but we begin to know his peace, more precious than any peace I can create for myself. On the other hand, our pain may be his pain, the pain of compassion at the suffering of the poor and voiceless of this world because of the greed, power-lust and arrogance of the strong. We cannot escape this pain, which is God's pain, and although we long to be free of it, we can find a peace and strength in it, and the will to combat it.

Spend a few minutes facing the fear of nuclear war. Look at Christ on the cross, as Salvador Dali depicts him, suspended over the globe of our world, now containing enough nuclear warheads to exterminate all life on earth forever. Speak to Christ. If you believe in the peace-giving value of the deterrent, tell him so as he hangs on the cross. If you deplore the deterrent, tell him of your loathing and ask him what you are to do. Let him be your teacher.

'Behold, I stand at the door and knock. If one of you hears me calling and opens the door, I will come in to share his meal, side by side with him' (Revelation 3:20). He is always there before me, beside me, above me, below me, within me, and he has, in St Catherine of Genoa's words, 'no other business but to unite himself to us.'

7.

Answering the call

Patrick Barry OSB

This book on prayer has brought to the surface issues concerning our deep response to God which are not just for Lent but for all time beyond it. Each contributor has rejected any idea that prayer is strictly for professionals or that it is a celestial game of snakes and ladders in which the ladders are for the mystics and the snakes for the rest of us.

There is nothing recommended in this book, no encouragement it gives, which does not apply equally to all the baptised. Baptism is the gateway to prayer, because it incorporates us into Christ. As we are all equal in baptism, so we are all equal in prayer – equal, that is, in the sense that the loving and unfailing invitation of God is equally to all at all times. In this sense prayer is the great ecumenical bond through which we can all learn to speak one language, whatever the divisions between Christians. And so, when Christians talk prayer, they inevitably converge; when they pray, a certain unity at the deepest level is already achieved.

I have often wondered why Vatican II did not include a treatise on prayer among the sixteen documents it issued. It is no answer to say that there are references to prayer in many of the other documents, as some have pointed out. Ecumenism and the liturgy and the role of bishops are mentioned in other documents, but that did not persuade the Council to exclude special documents on these subjects. Nor was I satisfied by the suggestion that the document on the liturgy covered all that needs to be said about prayer. Indeed, in speaking of the liturgy the Council itself seems almost to call for another treatise on prayer: 'The spiritual life, however, is not confined to participation in the liturgy. The Christian is assuredly called to pray with his brethren, but he must also enter into his chamber to pray to the Father in secret; indeed, according to the teaching of the Apostle Paul, he should pray without ceasing' (Constitution on the Liturgy, n. 12). Nor did I feel that, beneficial as the developments in liturgy have been since Vatican II, some of the more profound insights of the Council have been unequivocally reflected in the developing life of the Church today. 'It is of the essence of the Church,' says the Council in the Constitution on the Liturgy, 'that she be both human and divine, visible and yet invisibly endowed, eager to act and yet devoted to contemplation, present in this world and yet not at home in it. She is all these things in such a way that in her the human is directed and subordinated to the divine, the visible likewise to the invisible, action to contemplation and this present world to that city yet to come which we seek' (n. 2).

If it is true that we are all called to pray in secret as well as together, if action must be subordinated to contemplation, did we not need to hear more

about the meaning of contemplation in this context?
Are those stirring words at the beginning of the
document on the liturgy to be referred only to the
presence and importance of true contemplatives in
the life of the Church, or are they saying something
important about the quality of all Christian life in
a world of involvement and action? If we must all
find some way of realising St Paul's precept that we
should 'pray without ceasing', I could not help
thinking that an analysis of the meaning of Christian
prayer, a reminder of the more important aspects of
the Church's teaching and tradition on prayer
throughout the centuries would have been helpful,
especially if it had related that great tradition to the
changing needs and difficulties of modern life.

The most plausible explanation offered me for the
absence of the document which I should have
appreciated so much was that the Holy Spirit wanted
it that way. The Holy Spirit dwells in the hearts of
the faithful; was it, then, his work that inspired in
the years after the Council a great desire for prayer
and all sorts of theories and programmes to promote
it? The publication of books about prayer and books
of prayer became something of a growth industry.
Nor was it only within the Church that these movements appeared. The trail to the East was opened
up and thousands of young began to look for gurus,
of one sort or another, outside Christianity. Something was on; there were signs of a searching which
came from the heart. If I regretted that the Council
had not provided guidance drawn from the great
tradition of Christianity and applied it to life in the
modern world, I could not deny that something was

here – something perhaps as impressive as anything which certainly owed its origin to the Council. It arose, it seemed, from the hearts of the faithful, and who could find grounds to deny that it came from the Holy Spirit? Perhaps he wanted it that way – some things from the Council and some things from the hearts of the faithful.

When I read *The Easter People*, the bishops' response to the National Pastoral Congress of 1980, my thoughts were stirred once more by the comment that: 'Catholics ought to grow in a life of prayer and they have a right to expect their priests to teach them how to pray' (n. 66). They make the point in the context that there is no tension between liturgical prayer and private prayer and they both need each other. Many of the thoughts which had occurred to me earlier were given new colour and urgency. My work at the time brought me into contact with priests and religious and lay men and women in an urban setting. I noted how many there were for whom space in life and quiet and silence were virtually inaccessible from one end of the day to the other – from one end of the year to the other. I noted how increasingly busy is the life of priests and how difficult it is for them to find real space for prayer and how difficult to provide the ambience of prayer for the people. I wondered how and where they are to do this teaching and many of them, for one reason or another, seemed also baffled by this problem. Teaching prayer is not a matter of talks and lectures and academic exposition, nor is learning prayer a matter of study to be later applied in practice. To begin one's learning about prayer it is necessary to

begin to pray and even a perception of the most
important questions emerges only from constant
practice of prayer over quite a long period. This
must be so, because prayer is a deep personal
response to God, who takes the initiative through
our baptism in which 'the love of God', as St Paul
puts it, 'has been poured into our hearts.' We can
respond and gradually learn prayer's meaning and
grow in it, or we can allow ourselves to be distracted
from any real response because of 'the worries and
riches and pleasures of life'; in that case talk about
prayer means nothing – teaching about prayer is
ineffective.

It was all the more impressive, in view of the
difficulties, to find so much interest in prayer and
real perception and growth in prayer, often in very
unpromising circumstances. My impression grew,
however, that most of those who did achieve such
perception and growth owed much to retreat houses
where, they often said, they had discovered the
meaning of prayer for the first time. That is encouraging for those who can attend retreat houses, but
they are accessible only to the comparatively few
who have time and money, and by no means all of
them have the motivation to take their opportunities.
Moreover, those who had been to retreat houses
with great benefit often told me how difficult it was
when they returned home and no longer had the
support and inspiration they had found on their
retreat. For them continued growth in prayer is
difficult; for the others without their advantage it
may seem almost impossible.

How to make space in life for prayer was one

problem raised by the bishops' comment. The other
was concerned with the content of the teaching called
for. Granted that one must pray in order to learn
to pray, all experience through the ages shows that
guidance and help, and perhaps even more the
encouragement of others for whom prayer is part of
their lives, are needed on the way. Although I am
assured, and believe it to be true, that the Holy
Spirit has indeed inspired in the hearts of the faithful
the various developments in prayer life since the
Council, it does not follow that there are no problems
about these developments nor that everything is to
be taken as of equal value and validity. I am
reminded of a comment of Rahner's, when he suggests that theologians should recognise the work of
the Spirit 'even when it is evident that divine fire is
producing an awful lot of human smoke'. To cherish
the fire and distinguish it from the smoke requires
a lot of understanding which is firmly based on
Scripture and the continuing great tradition of the
Church.

The Council had made the point that liturgy is
not enough and had called attention to Christ's
teaching on prayer in secret in Matthew 6:6. As I
reflected on this and on the Council's other teaching
that Christ manifested his Father and himself by
words and deeds (cf. Constitution on Divine Revelation, *Dei Verbum,* n. 1), an enormous fact about
his deeds struck me. In the synoptic gospels (and
especially in Luke) he emerges emphatically as a
man who was always going off to pray by himself.
His experience in the desert and Gethsemane are
particularly familiar, but there are several other

references and the urgency of this habit of his is
given special emphasis in Luke 5:10: 'The crowds
would gather to hear him and have their sickness
cured, but he would always go off to some place
where he could be alone to pray.' Here at least was
a good start for those who were trying to follow
Christ. I thought I detected a hint of the same sort
of thing in his early followers in Acts 6:4, when the
apostles instituted the deacons in order that they
themselves might have time to continue to devote
themselves to 'prayer and service of the word'. The
order of priorities seemed to be significant. I wondered also whether Acts 10:9 contained the suggestion of a habit when 'Peter went to the housetop
about the sixth hour to pray'. The housetop, no
doubt, was the only place where he could be alone
in a Mediterranean town; the necessary time would,
of course, have to be found from his pressing occu-
pation of converting the whole world.

Today the same pattern does not seem to be
integral (even in aspiration) to the life of all the
faithful. In fact the idea of private prayer, which is
commended by Christ in words and deeds, is regrett-
ably seen by some to be in conflict with the imper-
atives of common prayer in the liturgy and concern
for social involvement and love of our neighbour
rather than for what is assumed to be personal and
private spiritual development. The problem here is
not just a question of balance leading to the conclu-
sion that a little private prayer, provided it does not
go too far, is a help to our involvement in prayer
and action with others. To solve the problem that
way is to miss a profound point about the true
meaning of what all prayer is in Christian life.

It is easy to think of prayer as an exercise to be carried out for the improvement (individual or collective) of our spiritual performance, like the exercise imposed by a physiotherapist. This is not a distortion but a contradiction of what Scripture and tradition proclaim. St Paul spoke of the Spirit helping our weakness: 'For we do not know how to pray as we ought, but the Spirit himself intercedes for us with sighs too deep for words. And he who searches the hearts of men knows what is the mind of the Spirit, because the Spirit intercedes for the saints according to the will of God' (Romans 8:26). St Augustine insists that when we pray it is Christ who prays in us and that it is essentially his prayer that we offer to the Father. Our prayer is never to be seen as our effort to bridge a chasm between creature and creator. Rather it is our surrender to the healing power which has already bridged it.

Therefore all prayer is one, whether it is in private or corporate mode, for it is our participation in the prayer of Christ through the Holy Spirit. Any conflict between individual and corporate prayer is simply illusory. It is also true that the one feeds the other both in the lives of individuals and in the life of the Church as a whole; and each needs the other. That is why the Council, speaking of contemplative religious communities, said: 'No matter how urgent may be the needs of the active apostolate, such communities will always have a distinguished part to play in Christ's Mystical Body, where all members have not the same function' (Decree on the Religious Life, n.7). The Council went on to insist of such contemplatives that 'by imparting a hidden apostolic fruitfulness they make God's people grow.'

It is desirable that prayer should be relevant to
life, but not that an activist approach to life should
be allowed to dominate and impoverish our prayer.
This relevance to life should refer not only to our
activity but also to the deeper strands of our consciousness in which we yearn for stillness. 'Be still
and know that I am God,' said the psalmist, and the
prayer in which we do this is not selfish any more
than Christ's solitary prayer was selfish. Since our
prayer derives what power and efficacy it has from
Christ in his risen life among us it has for its scope
his prayer for all mankind. That surely is why the
Council spoke of the prayer of contemplatives having
'a hidden apostolic fruitfulness'.

Techniques of meditation have become popular
since the Council. Many of these techniques have
been borrowed from the East and not all of them fit
readily into the Christian concept of what prayer
really is. It is possible to use these methods as a
means of self-improvement and self-control, which
is fine in its way, but we should be cautious of
identifying them with Christian prayer. The busy
executive may find that they are good for his blood
pressure and business acumen. The test is not this
sort of thing nor any supposed development of our
understanding of God and humanity and the world.
The test is in the deep response to God's love revealed
in Christ. 'By love he may be caught and held,' says
the *Cloud of Unkowing*, 'but by thinking never'
(ch. 6). There is no true prayer which is not a
surrender to his will and a willing stretching out to
his love. In this sense meditation is good and leads
us in the way of Christ's prayer. We need, at the

right time, to learn how to release ourselves from words and images and allow the Spirit to work in us at a deeper level. But we need also at this stage to remain alert in our will, for therein lies our active response to the Spirit.

Nor is the test of prayer to be found in emotional fulfilment. If there are times when we are blessed by feelings of emotional richness, if we get some glimpse in our lives of the importance of praise and thanksgiving and if we find expression of this, whether in pentecostal fervour or in deep silence, this is something to treasure and thank God for. But to seek to make emotion and feeling continuous and appropriate to all seasons (which it cannot be) is at best to risk imposing a strain on our inner credibility; at worst it may verge towards artifice and rob us of that direct simplicity in our approach to God which is so clearly embodied in the Our Father. There are times of emotional richness in prayer and times of involvement; there are times of perception and new light and times of peace; but there are also times of testing in faith. All the great teachers of prayer throughout the ages warn us of the times when darkness of one sort or another lies on the way of prayer, when we need lasting faith and perseverance and must not look for quick returns. These are times of purification, when we learn to adhere to God alone and cease to rely on the sense of satisfaction which can easily be so tainted with self-love. Faith and perseverance are the test, as Christ taught, and there are no techniques or programmes for avoiding that challenge.

As for petition, Christ commended it with some

emphasis but he added gently that the Father knows
better than we do what is good for us and left us in
no doubt that the bottom line in all petition is, 'Thy
will be done.' That is the *leitmotif* of his own life.
The purpose of petition is never to change God's
mind about anything (which is an absurdity) but to
change us ourselves and bring us nearer to God's
mind about us and how our lives should be both
here and hereafter. The great Christian writers
about prayer have never seen it as a means of
managing things so as to get our own way but as a
means whereby God gets his way with us to our
great benefit – at whatever cost.

Thus the most obvious and apparently simple
form of prayer in which we ask for things we want
or desperately need plunges us into the great mystery
of Christianity – that God loves mankind and that
men and women are called to respond with their
whole heart and soul and mind. God loves us too
much to contrive that we always have our own way.
Prayer is the means whereby he teaches us *his* way.
When our prayer is heard, as a prayer in faith
always is, what is given us is usually a change in
perspective – a new attitude and new strength to
enable us to deal with our problems; and that changes
the whole situation. Christ began his prayer in
Gethsemane by asking that his suffering might be
avoided, but he ended it with the prayer that his
Father's will might be accomplished. Then everything changed – for ever.

It is not programmes nor crash courses nor con-
gresses that are called for: We do not need motivators,
since the one and only motivator is the Holy Spirit

who 'dwells in the hearts of the faithful'. What is needed is that very simple but demanding change of heart by which we accept that it is of the very essence of our lives as Christians that, whatever our circumstances, whatever the complexities of our lives, we are all called to 'pray without ceasing'.